About the Author

The heart of marketing professional and poet, Raquelle Puglisi, can be found somewhere on a park bench in New York City. Or maybe under a tiny little light on a tiny little street, writing a tiny little passage for you. For the last decade, she's been writing poems and making an impact in the marketing world for companies like IBM, AMC Networks, and Coach. She is a role model for the fighters of the world, for the lovers, the strong willed and the girls who have been there. Wherever she goes, people know they don't need to try to be somebody else.

They're already good enough.

Tiny Passages to Pass the Time

Raquelle Puglisi

Tiny Passages to Pass the Time

Olympia Publishers
London

www.olympiapublishers.com
OLYMPIA PAPERBACK EDITION

Copyright © Raquelle Puglisi 2023

The right of Raquelle Puglisi to be identified as author of this work has been asserted in accordance with sections 77 and 78 of the Copyright, Designs and Patents Act 1988.

All Rights Reserved

No reproduction, copy or transmission of this publication may be made without written permission.
No paragraph of this publication may be reproduced, copied or transmitted save with the written permission of the publisher, or in accordance with the provisions of the Copyright Act 1956 (as amended).

Any person who commits any unauthorised act in relation to this publication may be liable to criminal prosecution and civil claims for damage.

A CIP catalogue record for this title is available from the British Library.

ISBN: 978-1-80074-586-5

This is a work of fiction.
Names, characters, places and incidents originate from the writer's imagination. Any resemblance to actual persons, living or dead, is purely coincidental.

First Published in 2023

Olympia Publishers
Tallis House
2 Tallis Street
London
EC4Y 0AB

Printed in Great Britain

Dedication

These words are for the misfit toys of the world. May they help you feel a little less lonely.

Acknowledgements

To the boy who broke my heart, to the man who helped me put it back together, and to the girls — oh, the girls. Without you, I wouldn't have this book. Thank you.

can you breathe now?

i know my love was suffocating,
and i used to want to apologize for that.
but i don't feel sorry for,
reminding you how great you were,
or how proud i was,
or how good you looked when you woke up.
can you breathe now?
take a deep breath.
that is simplicity.
that is everything i'm not.

time is like medicine

i placed you on a pedestal,
so high i couldn't reach you.
but as time passes,
i care less about making you feel shitty,
and more about making you disappear.
everything is brighter with you gone.
you left a trail of gloom in every room you visited.
i don't know what it was about you,
but i'm so glad i can't remember.
time is like medicine,
and i think i finally kicked you.

the prints on the wall

i knew you were different,
when i touched your face.
i was lighter with you,
higher with you,
without a single sip of wine.
i saw you through your camera lens,
and focused on your hands.
moving up and down my legs,
inside the pockets of my jeans.
you saw me,
how i saw you.
a rare moment of acceptance,
that i didn't know i longed for.
there was a sense of power in being alone,
but you made me want to stay.
you were the headline we were waiting for,
the good news after the bad,
the gift you asked for,
but never got.
the prints on the wall.
the weird,
and the wild.
the complicated,
and the confusing.

the queen of the down

place that fast food crown on my head,
because i will always be the queen of the down.
the hardest to love,
but you keep me around.

the seatbelt sign is on

how is it that points on a map,
could make you feel more than human touch?
an overpacked suitcase stationed above your seat,
flying over millions of people,
people unphased by an oversized piece of metal,
floating gracefully above.
the seatbelt sign is on.
feels like his hands around your waist.
the sights you see,
like paint on a canvas,
or music on the subway to work.
drowning out the bad,
with something much more beautiful.
something that was always there,
but it's your turn to really see.

she's alright

the fog in my brain has become a permanent resident,
retracing thoughts or movements i made earlier that day.
i am symbolically picking at pieces of my brain with a knife.
blood drips down my face.
it's warm but i am cold,
freezing to touch in the middle of august.
if my hands stop listening to my thoughts,
how will i touch you?
how will i tell you what i feel if i can't remember to feel it?
i am sorry i am fading.
will you forgive me when i go,
even if i'm still here?
brain on fire,
but they say she's alright.

the broken gps

you hate me for loving you so much.
i hate me for loving you so much.
you're freezing to touch,
yet my arms are wide open.
"how did we get here?"
i asked.
even though i knew you led us this way.
i just really wish you would have asked me for directions.

all the colors

when you told me you had something for me,
i thought you were enough.
then we drank coffee by the rain,
with the music all the way up.
not everyone is good,
because it's harder that way.
but you're made of all the colors,
that make me want to stay.

the sad sun

a dark room,
pale skin.
the weather is changing again.
a sad song,
about love.
they make it sound so easy.
the hard days,
seem long.
but it's the sun who let us down.
all that pressure,
to stay up,
even when it wants to frown.

checkups are good for your health

i still check up on you from time to time,
just to make sure you're okay.
you were my childhood,
my heart on a silver platter.
the love doesn't disappear,
just because you did.
do you feel it too?
we could build cities,
as long as we're apart.

jump in

i drank too much wine again,
but it feels good,
to feel lifeless.
life is hard,
and serious,
because i guess it would bore us,
if not.
the boy i loved in high school,
taught me to be different.
he said it would be fun,
but now my head is heavier than my heart,
and it doesn't feel strong,
like it should.
i don't have much more to give,
but they tell me i should be okay,
in a few more days.
it's always that way.
a few days of darkness,
is okay until it gets old,
and everyone has their sunglasses on,
because they say it's pretty sunny,
and the waters warm,
and just cut it out,
and jump in.

more today

in the midst of everything,
i can't stop being selfish.
and i feel sorry,
but not sorry enough,
to make it stop.
i'll watch the whole world burn down,
while still wondering if you love me,
more today,
than yesterday.

close calls

there were a few close calls before this.
the weather held up,
or my love would grow big.
i'm sorry for the urgency,
i thought that this was it.
but every time i go to leave,
you are what i miss.

the rolling stones

he spoke with absolutely no doubt.
he was so sure of himself,
so completely aware of his surroundings.
it was attractive,
almost too attractive.
he had the ability to look straight past me,
straight through me.
we were talking,
engaging conversation,
but he didn't hear me,
he didn't see me,
and when his lips touched mine,
i couldn't help but think,
he was the kind of guy,
who chose the rolling stones over the beatles.

the falls

my hands are tired from scratching your back,
stroking your ego,
gripping your throat.
my mouth waters as i look at your lips.
they move,
and you talk,
but i'm not listening.
you are the one i'd call in a hurry.
i'd like to take you with me on a drive to the falls,
but i wouldn't know what to say.
the temperature is rising,
but my patience is thinning.
when i kiss you again?
will your eyes stay shut?
if i had to name you,
i'd call you my greatest tragedy.
the one that could burn down the city,
but i forgot my light.

more than a poem

before you,
i wrote about them.
and after you,
i'll write about them.
but you are different.
and a poem is not enough,
to express what i feel for you.
i promise not to spill my guts on paper with pen,
but to give you what i feel,
for all the time that i can.

drunk dancing

let's get drunk,
and dance in the kitchen.
talk about the world,
and all that it's missing.
we have so much time,
to be anywhere else.
i just feel so good with you,
as myself.

mason jar

it wasn't something you could teach.
it wasn't something you could buy.
i wasn't sure how to feel,
or to feel at all.
i wanted to hold on to it.
place it in a mason jar.
open it on occasion,
to remind myself,
that today,
i reached out and touched it.
real,
genuine,
happiness.

a love so grand

i gave you the love that i deserved.
the biggest love.
a love so grand.

ghost

i may never sleep.
my heart is beating through my shirt.
i keep replaying every word you said,
just to get to the bottom of where you went.
you pulled a sheet over your head,
cut two holes for eyes,
and said you weren't a ghost.

writer's block

rode the train this morning,
and it felt nostalgic.
tried to write something,
but nothing came to me.
been in my feelings,
about always feeling.
and the doors keep opening,
but i'm sitting still.
got you on my mind,
for years now.
and it's nice to know,
it hasn't dimmed.
want to show you everything,
i ever loved.
and make sure,
you always fit in.

cold

it was weird because i let it be.
i cried for two weeks straight.
i felt myself falling,
tumbling,
into a deep dark rabbit hole,
with no promise of wonderland.
we played music because it was nostalgic.
we took pictures because we could.
so much love to give,
but your arms were crossed,
and your face was tight.
at a loss for words i asked if you needed a sweater.
i wasn't sure what the point was.
but i still wonder if it pays to be that cold.

gold eye shadow

i put on gold eye shadow today,
hoping it would make me feel something.
and i think it worked,
but i can't really be sure.
most days are like all the other days,
and i don't feel bad about it.
i guess i just want to know,
if i'm doing my part.
like if i was measured by my kindness,
would that be enough?
or would i bury my head into a pillow,
and wonder what else i could have done?

hysteria

the earth is screaming,
but this time it's coming from the people.
they can hear us in outer space now.
even as we sit in silence,
with hysteria written on our foreheads.

new york city

we fell hard,
before we knew what to call it.
it felt strange to love a city,
like a person.
the lights could blind the others,
but here we are,
one city,
yet a worlds away from simplicity.

words of affirmation

i am the night sky,
in an open field.
a quick trip from the city,
an escape from the fog.
the tiny stars,
with big beauty.
how they tell me,
i should feel.
i am the night sky,
in an open field.
repeating,
and repeating,
until it finally feels real.

we all got the blues

we'll go on talking about it forever,
always printed on the backs of our brains.
the year,
it felt heavy and painful.
shielding the sun with all of our shade.
i feel so sorry for the first timers.
it's not easy when,
we all got the blues.
the color was calm and inviting,
until now,
it felt like it should.
i lay on the grass,
and keep silent.
counting the clouds,
that pass through.
it's true,
that it's got to all of us.
even the sky's got it too.

a sunday that doesn't feel scary

what does it say about those,
who love so hard,
the ones who love so small?
longing for something that doesn't exist,
in someone who appears to exist,
but it feels extinct.
of special value,
like a vintage handbag in perfect condition,
or a sunday that doesn't feel scary.
it's okay to feel more than others,
to feel more for others.
the intensity is right.
it just belongs to you,
not them.

a stranger i knew so well

last night,
i saw you for the first time in a long time.
i wanted to run into your arms and hug you,
tell you all the things you missed,
tell you it's okay what we did.
but you wouldn't look at me.
it was a chilling feeling to have you there,
a stranger i knew so well.

he was a man

i reached for my clothes when we were done,
but he threw them across the room.
he grabbed me and pulled me close,
and kissed my entire body.
how could he look me in the eyes when he fucked me,
if he didn't want me to see right through him?
we faked love for a night,
and it felt so good.
this wasn't about you.
this came after you.
he was a man,
and you'll always be a little boy.

my hero

the clock is spinning,
my head is too.
this all feels too familiar.
i don't want to fall again.
it's just too hard to get back up.
but then there's you.
my hero,
you pull me back.
a superpower they don't make movies about.

the same shade of red

walking through the city,
people on every corner.
human hearts beating at different speeds.
the shade of red changing as we inhale and exhale.
i loved you when we met,
knew this was forever.
comparing scars like it's going out of style.
you work so hard,
to appear so strong.
but you are stronger than you think,
and more beautiful than you feel.
a vision,
a fresh roll of film,
a lazy sunday afternoon.
i get you like you get me.
the same shade of red.

paris

love me like i love paris.
like the words dancing off their lips,
like the romance that screams,
and the romance that whispers.
like the lights that flicker,
and the poems that sing.
love me like i love paris.
so i can feel it,
even when you're not here.

one hundred miles

a baby is sitting next to me on the subway,
and i can't help but wonder what his eyes have seen.
we grow up so quickly with the stickiest of memories,
glued to the backs of our eyelids.
and you wonder why you dreamt about the guy you kissed
nine years ago,
who wasn't even a good kisser.
or the medication you used to take to make you feel
happy.
or the food you wished you didn't eat,
but had to eat.
if i have love in my heart,
is that enough to get me through the bad stuff?
the bad stuff that comes back after it hibernated for
months.
what do you see when you lay in bed?
covers to your neck,
kind of feel like his hands clasping tight.
when you play with me it's like recess again.
no one feels like you do.
we all don't see like you do.
i'd run one hundred miles just to see me like you do.

the problem with sleeping

i wake in the middle of the night,
patting the right side of the bed,
hoping to feel your skin again.
but all i feel is linen.
that's the problem with sleeping.

heartbreak kids

it's so fun to sing about heartbreak.
we're all screaming rhymes now.
what's all the fuss?
like we didn't want to die,
when it was us.
and i'm running in circles,
about how far i've come.
and how far she's come.
and he's come.
and we've come.
singing about heartbreak.
the shared trauma,
that we all came from.

skyscraper love

i have never been loved so vividly,
with pure focus and intention.
my heart beats the same rhythm that you sang to me,
in the car when you didn't think i was listening.
even when i was little,
chaos seemed to find me,
because i told it to stay.
but if every day was as big as those skyscrapers,
i'd never know you could make me feel this way.

quiet on the rollercoaster

i don't know what i'm talking about,
but people believe that i do.
i still feel sad when good things happen,
because eventually they fall through.

old friend

did you know,
if you killed me back then,
i'd get so good at being alive,
now?
isn't it funny how it all worked out?
this is a letter,
for an ex-lover,
turned friend,
in my head.
i know we don't speak,
but i want you to know,
what you did for me,
back then,
oh,
it made me so much better,
now.

sad girls

it'll be so bad,
if this was all for nothing.
i don't feel good again.
should i say something?
i'm always so sorry,
to interrupt your day,
with all of the fucking shit i say.
roaming through my thoughts,
i found a reminder,
from the last time i felt at fault.
things get better,
i think it said.
from one sad girl,
to another,
on a different day.

like they say in the movies

i still hope that we get a moment,
to sit down and talk.
about everything that happened,
after our life fell apart.
it's always so silly to care,
about what's gone.
but i know you know better,
to think i've done you wrong.
i'm sorry i wrote such horrible things.
but grieving a loss,
is hard to forgive.
i wish you the best,
like they say in the movies.
because without you,
i would have never,
found all of this beauty.

like watering the plants

gotta cry it out,
like watering the plants.
just think,
it's impossible to grow,
with all that sun.
maybe today hasn't been your day,
for a few days.
but when you're all out of water,
i think the clouds will go their own way.

cloudy

if we're going to keep doing this,
can i at least get some sleep?
it's like the days don't quit,
making me feel ashamed.
and i owe myself an apology,
for the dark colors i painted.
let the clouds follow me around,
until those sad colors faded.
and you can keep telling me i'm broken,
but i think it's kind of funny,
how together i can be,
to get you to notice me.
if pieces of me break off,
i think that's the whole story.
how tall i can stand,
with all that behind me.

nice to meet you, again

if i was locked in a tiny room,
with no view,
maybe i could see myself,
for the first time,
in months.
i see everything else,
and i mark it all in my brain,
as a way to be.
a check on the list,
that was drafted a million years ago.
this place is everything but free,
and it's strange to feel lost within your own body.
i can touch my face,
but it doesn't feel familiar.
i don't know myself any more.
i don't see myself any more,
for the person that people love,
or the person that i was proud to be.

notes

i'm writing this down,
to remember this feeling,
when it feels like it's so far away.
and if you find me lost in all those feelings,
i just ask that you tell me to stay.

no title

stripped away from my title,
i felt lonely in my thoughts,
and tired in my face.
they say what you do defines you,
but what about how you do it?
i guess,
not everything is poetic,
or profound.
to grieve a loss that is not a person,
feels funny to some.
but you can lose something you love,
and learn it's okay to still love something you lost.

feel

i'm sorry i'm always talking about how i feel.
it's almost like,
it makes it feel real.
when life is a blur,
and we're always in a rush,
it makes me feel better to tell you what's up.
i get that the talking is a lot to take in,
and if this was a competition,
i'd be sure to win.
i just can't help but apologize for all that i feel.
i want to turn it off,
but i feel and i feel.
it's crazy there's people who let it pass by,
without a worry or question or even a try.
i've always admired the loose and the lazy,
but if i had to choose,
i think i'd still pick this crazy.
i write a lot of poems,
and i talk a lot of shit,
but it only feels good,
if you're with me through it.

one hundred love songs

i'd like to write a book,
about how good you look.
three chapters dedicated,
to the rings on your fingers,
or the way you sip your cocktail.
i'd write you one hundred love songs,
if i could sing like you,
even though you tell me you're no good.
i'll keep trying to sum it all up,
but i'm scared i'll fall flat.
i guess it's just,
loving you is easy,
with a face like that.

like the clouds knew

on thursday i sat in the car,
while you were inside.
it rained,
and it rained.
it was almost like the clouds knew,
that i was all out of tears.
they did all the work for me.
and i just closed my eyes,
and let someone else take care of me.

the lovelandtown bridge

the other day i drove past a bridge,
in a town that i grew up in,
that for the first time in my life,
i read the name.
the lovelandtown bridge.
why did it matter to me now?
i drove past it so many times before.
a name like that,
longs for a moment,
published in a book,
or played in a movie.
and i'm writing about it,
as if something really special happened there,
but it didn't.

lockdown

a lot of people are alone,
again.
trapped in four walls.
in a city that taught us,
home is,
where you go,
what you see,
and with who.
not in a bed,
in an overpriced room.

unexpected romance

sitting on the floor,
eating sushi,
is more romantic than it sounds.

red

i tried to dye my hair red,
but it wouldn't stick.
i thought maybe it meant something,
but now i don't think it did.

the sad and the sorry

"you always make everyone feel so good,"
she said.
"but what about me?"
i thought.
i'm home again.
back in the thick aired dark place.
are you tired of reading about it?
because i'm tired of writing about it.
as cold as it is,
it still feels warm and fuzzy,
to know what comes next.
i am so good at this.
the sad and the sorry.
the depressed and the damaged.

drunk drive home

it was that drunk drive home,
that made me feel alone.
and i wanted to write this down,
but i couldn't find my phone.
and it felt like he still didn't get it,
but i told him so many times.
that love isn't love,
without you by my side.

the perfectly painted

she painted a picture of him,
with colors that sang.
a ballad of his life,
and all that he's made.
forever he stood,
on the tallest pedestal,
in her heart.
a place that he'll stay,
even now
further apart.

skinny heart

if i eat a little less,
will my heart finally feel full?
if i work out a little harder,
will my days get easier?
i've read so many self-help books,
that never actually teach me a lesson.
and it's been years of me begging myself,
to stop obsessing over my reflection.
they say watch your weight,
but there is so much more to see,
in a world of comparisons,
that just won't let me be.

distance is a hell of a come down

i sprint through my dreams in search of you.
count down the days until we're together again.
when you're not here,
i remember what it was like,
before you painted my life the boldest of colors.
distance is a hell of a come down.

the city in slow motion

dead flowers taped to the wall,
on display to give them a longer life.
they deserved more than six days of attention.
a summer afternoon with the blinds shut tight.
as hard as i tried,
it was impossible to find comfort in misery.
this was all so new.
i sat up and reached for my phone,
rereading the messages,
we exchanged the night before.
his voice on repeat in my head.
it felt so good to feel so good.
to feel excited about something,
that didn't make much sense.
the mystery of him made my legs weak.
in my mind he traced my tattoos with his fingers.
the walls were singing now.
my hands moved slowly down my body.
he wasn't here,
yet he lit up the room.
he was the coffee on the way to work.
the flowers on the wall.
the city in slow motion.

tired

oh man,
you're tired.
damn,
you got me.
i'm sleeping now.
pieces of my hair on the floor,
pieces of my hair in the creases of your fingers.
why'd you have to be so tough?
we ruined each other,
because it was so fucking easy.
your face is too pretty,
because it probably belongs to someone else.
i don't think of you.
i won't think of you.
i'm thinking of you.
damn,
you got me.
you're tired.
i'm tired.
so tired,
from chasing you around.

pep talks in the mirror

stay dark even in the brightest light.
fight the fight,
with no opponent.
get high off of being alone.
kiss like winter,
chill your bones.
tell yourself it's okay to be sorry,
for wishing for another body.
you are more than a shell of a good heart.
you are more than a fresh start.
the curves of your body,
they won't fail you.
they don't define you.
the lengths they take just to hide you.
the marathons you run just to find you.
pep talks in the mirror,
with a side of desire to please,
everyone but the person staring back.

the skinny man

he seemed fearless.
super careless.
i guess it was hard for me to get why everyone was so quiet,
about something so loud.
this time was different.
he didn't look at me when i spoke to him.
physically he stood tall,
but he appeared small.
i don't think his days were ever easy,
even if they could have been.
he didn't like easy.
i watched him from a far,
as his fidgety hands tapped on the kitchen table.
he was going to leave the party.
but where would he go?
he always wanted more.
but there wasn't anything else we could give him.
so they watched and waited,
for the skinny man to leave.
so they could talk about him,
in the corner of the living room.

they're calling for rain

there were years where we had so much to say.
but today,
we talked about the weather,
and i knew in that moment,
it was over.
i wanted to forget that it happened.
we both brushed it off so quickly.
but tonight before bed,
i just laid there,
my eyes as swollen as the clouds above my head.
it wasn't my fault.
you can't force love to stay.
but i still wished so badly,
that i didn't ask him if it was going to rain on sunday.

YOU ARE
THE FIRE

you are the fire

i don't know anyone like you.
you are the grass that is greener.
you are the diamond in the rough.
you are the gold jewelry that hangs from my neck,
clasped tight enough to make me feel something,
but you still let me breathe.
you are the quiet and the crazy.
you are the feeling right before,
and directly after.
you are the poetry and the irony.
my fingers through your hair.
the movie playing on the wall.
you are the cool side of the pillowcase,
and at the same time,
you are the fire.

we all get sad club

if you are always so good,
why do i feel so bad?
i'll love you for a lifetime,
but i can't promise i won't be sad.
it's like the world,
how it spins,
even when it rains and snows.
or how we go on in life,
without the touch of our loved ones.
i'd like to start a club,
where we go when we get sad.
a place where the others aren't allowed.
the come down,
the spiral,
the rain that's not pouring from the clouds.
the bad days,
the sad days,
the clothes in the lost and found.

like you do

i'm sorry for what i said,
when you told me i was mean.
it's just that,
some days i paint this really dark picture,
that the whole world is out to get me.
like if i was to stand on the tippy top of the empire state
building,
and look down,
that i would see a sea of people,
so angry at me.
and they would stomp,
and yell,
and tell my secrets.
and i would look down,
and plead my case,
try to explain why i feel what i feel,
try to get them to like me,
like i should like me.
and they would stand there all day,
like they had all the time in the world,
to hate me.
but there you go,
reminding me that,
no one really cares,

like you do.
and people who do really care,
will let you know,
let you feel it,
like you do.
and the people who really matter,
will help you see,
like you do.

a town by the airport

we lived in a town by the airport.
like ocean waves on a sound machine,
or christmas music on the first day of december.
i laid in bed in a town by the airport.
they felt so close,
but it didn't feel scary.
i would wonder where they were going,
or hope it was you coming back from your trip.
i miss the sound of the airplanes.
swishing through the air,
that we breathe in for survival.
traveling away,
or home.
big bulky airplanes,
they'd dance.
so elegantly,
like a ballerina on stage.

how are you today?

does your heart bleed,
or beat?
you'd think,
it'd be easy to say you're fine,
if you feel fine.
what's it going to take to feel good,
when everything is going better than good?
how are you today?
do you feel enough,
or a little?
do you feel anything at all?
why are we always asking,
when we never actually reply,
with what we want to say?

forever was a fad anyway

nothing was more ironic,
than the tattoos plastered across his body.
a dictionary on his nightstand,
with a missing page for the word forever.
he felt good,
until he felt bad.
he was mine,
until he wasn't.
pulled out that crumbled page from his back pocket,
and grabbed her hand instead.
time would pass,
and i would wonder where i fit.
then there was this guy who felt like he'd stick.
losing track of time,
leaving our watches at home,
didn't need a dictionary for what we had.
i'd burn all the dictionaries for what we had.
forever was a fad anyway.

the man with the money

i don't know you,
or where you've been.
there is a stain on your suit,
and your hair is unfit.
the subway is buzzing,
and so is my brain.
i looked at you,
because you appeared to be sane.
you didn't let anyone beg,
you didn't let anyone sing.
you placed your hand in your wallet,
so unafraid.
i think the homeless considered you their friend,
even if you were gone,
and they would never see you again.

liar liar

i hugged him goodbye.
i didn't want to let go,
but i knew i had to.
i was always giving.
he was always taking.
i still wanted to give him one last thing.
something to leave him with.
i looked up at him.
i was always so tiny in his arms.
i stared into his eyes.
they didn't look at me with love any more.
i wondered,
what can you give someone who has everything?
i told him i would love him forever.
he said he was sorry.
i knew i wouldn't love him forever.
it just felt so good to give him the gift of that lie.

the city in the summer

it was almost like he wasn't listening,
but it was monday,
so i'm pretty sure no one was listening.
i stepped out from my apartment,
and looked down at my shoes.
they were tied so tightly.
water trickled down,
and landed on the top of my head.
i thought how cool it was that it was finally raining.
the city in the summer,
was starting to wear on us all.
i walked a couple steps,
realizing those few hopeful drops of water,
came from the old air conditioner stationed up above.
it belonged to the man on the fifth floor.
he was unhappy.
i was disappointed.

the morning prisoner

my crown is broken,
from stomping on it every morning.
should i dress myself in the dark?
i wondered.
my fingers touch every inch of my body.
the indents in my legs,
the emptiness in my heart,
for myself,
but so full for everyone else.
all these years,
and i still feel like a stranger.
a prisoner,
in a body i don't want.

the airport

all around me,
i see people who also feel shitty from time to time.
these people,
they talk.
they smile.
they sit.
they walk.
a baby is crying,
because she doesn't know what everyone is saying to her.
she is tiny and her parents are tired.
across the way,
a man in a tall hat is reading a copy of helter skelter.
like a car crash on the side of the road,
or a movie about heartbreak,
why do we love to find comfort in misery?
i probably don't want to know their sorrows.
no one wants to know mine.
i believe in tomorrow.
so do they.
so we continue on in life,
and in the airport.

playing pretend

when the world is ending,
and if i got you,
the thunder doesn't feel so scary,
and the news starts to blend and blur,
into words that i can't hear,
but still run true.
when the world is ending,
and if i got you,
it doesn't feel so bad.
under the covers,
we can play pretend,
like a steel fort,
that's built for this type of tragedy.

because

because you loved me,
before i loved me.
and you tell me it's okay to be sad,
instead of stop being sad,
or why are you sad?
because even when you can't listen,
you want to listen.
because your hand always finds a way to remind me that
you're here.
because you're here,
even when you're not here.
because you're patient,
and so much more than i'd ever imagine you'd be.
full of life,
and struggle,
and so much to see.
because you're warm,
and you're cool,
and you're safe,
but in a way that you feel like home,
and not in a way that you drive under the speed limit.
because you make me laugh when i'm mad.
and when we kiss,
we fly high.

because you want to learn,
but love to teach.
because your face,
and your feet,
and everything in between.
because when i feel small,
you make sure i feel seen.

things

i want to tell you so many things.
but you're gone,
and i don't think you're coming back.
i hope she tells you so many things,
because i'm gone,
and i can't come back,
because you won't let me in.

the lady and her land

was she stuck in space?
on a different planet?
her life was falling apart,
but she laughed all day,
and let the hurt happen over and over.
she didn't seem phased by it all.
this was the life she chose,
so she wasn't going anywhere,
even though it felt like she was always somewhere else.
some might say there wasn't much left to live for,
but she was filled with life.
an umbrella on a rainy day.
where did she go?
could we come along?
the lady and her land.
population one.

cold coffee

you're kind of like cold coffee.
with a plan to warm me up,
wake me up,
make me feel like i can take on the day.
your intention was good,
you're just not right.

golden girl

when i think of you,
i think of gold.
the shade of jewelry,
that dangles from your arms,
your ears,
your neck.
the color of your heart,
your brain,
your fingers wrapped around mine.
you are the one that radiates,
the one that shines.
the one that needed nothing,
and gave everything,
every single time.
fly high,
golden girl,
paint the sky the purest shade.
we'll go on loving you wherever we go.
please don't be afraid.

for the weak ones

weights strapped to my ankles at your front door.
warning signs painted across your chest,
yet i still feel safe.
i tell you to leave me be,
and yet you still welcome me.
you're not for the faint of heart.
you're not for the weak ones.
why's it so tough to stay away?
told my heart to take it easy,
going to listen to my head today.
it's always a fight.
a battle they'll write about in history books.

small

i was always so sure i could fly.
my arms wouldn't quit.
i wouldn't let them eat me alive.
i would stand in the center of that city,
and still feel tall.
but when your words cut me like a knife,
i feel so fucking small.

the man with the mermaids

he stood by the water,
while we played in the sand.
he didn't believe in magic,
but he told us about the mermaids.
every day was a flip of a coin with him.
what side was he going to be?
when he stood alone,
i wanted to join him,
but i never did.
he is now learning how to feel.
it didn't ever come easy for him.
without his mask,
he is scared.
in those moments when i see him shake,
i want to take him back to the ocean,
where everything was simple,
and he could be the man with the mermaids.

you did good, kid

"you did good, kid."
i mouthed to my nephew,
after successfully jumping to the next pillow.
a classic game of the floor is lava,
to remind you how much you've grown.
it wasn't as easy as i remembered,
but i still made it.
"you did good, kid."
i thought to myself.

Printed in the USA
CPSIA information can be obtained
at www.ICGtesting.com
JSHW020522301123
52802JS00002B/89